YOGA GAMES AND ACTIVITIES
VOLUME 1

Yoga Games and Activities Volume 1

FIRST EDITION

Yoga Games and Activities Volume 1 is written and self-published by Jan Pratt.

ISBN: 9798988793625

Dedicated to Our Children

the ones we taught,

have yet to meet,

and the ones we raised.

Acknowledgments

I am thankful for all the students who have learned with me over the years, all the parents who have entrusted their children to the practices of yoga, and the many mentors who have taught me the yoga path.

Namaste

Yoga Tools for Kids:
Creating Healthy Minds & Bodies Series

- ❖Yoga Breath Practices
- ❖Yoga Games & Activities Volume 1
- ❖Yoga Games & Activities Volume 2
- ❖Mindfulness & Meditation for Children
- ❖Yoga Lesson Plans for Kids
- ❖Mantra Affirmation Cards

Make each day your master piece!

John wooden

Table of Contents

Ball Pass with Feet

Chocolate Games

Rocket or Volcano

Kindness Hearts

Spell Your Name

Bean Bag Name Game

Creating a Show

Design a Pose

Eye Gazing

Gratitude Journal

Group Counting

Minute to Win It Games

Peace Flags

PracticeTeaching

Rolling Wave Teen/Tween

Game Service Projects

Thorn, Bud, Rose

YOGA GAMES AND ACTIVITIES

VOLUME 1

Yoga Games and Activities

Volume 1

For School Agers and Teens/Tweens

Activities that you can use to teach yoga skills: focus, patience, creativity and connection to others.

YOGA GAMES AND ACTIVITIES FOR SCHOOL AGERS

ACTIVITIES FOR SCHOOL AGE

ADD A POSE

A FUN GAME THAT ALLOWS FOR GROUP PARTICIPATION

AND

WILL GET IN A LOT OF YOGA!

Start standing in a circle.
Pick someone to start the game - often the teacher.
Pick a pose to demonstrate and then everyone does it with you. Move to the next person and they name a pose. Now, everyone does the first pose and then the second pose. Continue around the circle, adding a pose and then doing the whole sequence of poses.

Variation 1
You can turn this game into a name game also.
Everyone says each person's name as they do the sequence of poses.

Variation 2
After everyone has had a turn, try to do the poses in reverse order.

Games for School Age

Barrel of Monkeys

THIS GAME CAN BE FOUND ONLINE AND IN YOUR LOCAL DOLLAR STORES OR WALMARTS

Have everyone sit in a circle.
Take the monkeys from the barrel and toss them in a pile in the middle of the circle.
The goal is to pick up a new monkey by only holding onto the hand of the first monkey.
If you get a monkey, then you pass it on to the next person. If the monkey falls off, pull a yoga card and everyone does the pose on the card, while the monkey holder does the pose while holding the monkeys! Hopefully, none fall off!
After the pose, the next person gets to try.
Continue around the circle until everyone has had a turn.

There are many set that are available. This deck is by 'I Am Yoga.'

Games for School Age

It's a Balancing Act

Material: spoon and large marshmallow, Hersey kiss, or a none-food item like a ping-pong ball or large pompom

This game requires focus and attention to try and keep the marshmallow on the spoon as you move through poses. The hardest poses to complete will be poses that require bending forward or moving from the floor to standing or vice versa.
Inadvertently, this is also an exercise for the jaw!

Directions

Have everyone stand on their mats and pass out the plastic spoons. Demonstrate how everyone is going to hold the handle of the spoon in the mouth safely. You don't want the handle to poke anyone's mouth by placing it too far toward the back of the mouth. When everyone has this process down, have them remove the spoons and give their jaw a rest while you give directions.
Pass out the item that is going to be held on the spoon. Tell everyone that when you say go, they will put the spoon in their mouth, and place the item on the spoon as they are standing in mountain pose. Then, you will give directions to do different poses. The goal is to keep the item balanced on the spoon as they move through the different poses.
If the item falls off, students just pick it up and place it back on the spoon.

Courtesy of Janice Pratt

Games for School Age

Penguin Game

PENGUINS ALL HAVE A UNIQUE CALL.

THIS IS AWAY FOR THEM TO FIND MATES AND CHILDREN.

Sit with a long, tall spine.
Think of a unique sound you can make so that all your friends will be able to recognize you just from this sound.
On the count of 3, have everyone make their sound. Now let's try that sound using a full breath. Take a deep breath in and then as you exhale, make your sound.
Repeat two more times.

Penguin Sound Game

Now that everyone has their sound have students get in pairs. Have them share their sound. Decide which partner will go first. When the bell rings, everyone will close their eyes and bring their arms out in front of them. They will slowly start moving around the room, using their arms to keep them safe. When the next bell rings, one partner of each pair will make their unique sound. Partners will try to find each other just by using their hearing!

Games for School Age

TOE – GA

Material: pompom balls, marbles or glass breads

This game is fun for all ages, especially for school agers. Little kids may need to use their hands to pick up the pompoms. Older kids may not want to take off their shoes.

This game is about strengthening the feet which will help with balance.

Directions

Place yoga mats in a circle.

Place a pile of pompoms in the middle of the circle.

Tell everyone that this game is for their feet only. No hands allowed.

When the music starts, everyone will kindly go to the middle and grab some pompoms with their toes.

They will then take the pompoms to the back end of their mat and drop them there.

Keep picking up pompoms until the music stops.

When the music stops, have everyone line the pompoms they picked up at the front of the mat.

At this point, you can have kids count their pompoms, if you are going to play again or you can leave them in a line on the front of the mat.

I try to encourage this as non-competitive. You are just trying to make your toes strong. Now, have everyone lay on their bellies and blow the pompoms back into the middle.

Repeat if you have time.

Toe-Ga variations" continued

Variation 1

Using different types of items to pick up with your feet.
Marbles, small toys, feathers.
Use your imagination.

Variation 2

When they carry the pompoms back to their mat, have them put the pompoms in a small bucket.

Variation 3

Keep track of the number of items you pick up, and brainstorm ways that you can get better.
For example: using both feet or going faster.

Variation 4

Add a yoga pose like crab walk or airplane to the game. They have to stay in the pose the best they can while moving back and forth to their mat.

ACTIVITIES FOR SCHOOL AGES

WHERE IS THE STAR?

Materials: mats, paper stars

Materials: mats, paper stars

This game is about tapping into your intuition. Can you figure out which mat the star is under just by listening to your gut feelings?

Directions

Have students sit on their yoga space or at desks. Ask one student to volunteer to step out of the room. Tell the class that you are going to hide a star or other shape under someone's mat while the volunteer is out of the room.

When the volunteer comes back in, everyone is going to think about where the star is and the volunteer is going to try to figure out where the star is hidden. Take turns until the game feels done.

When the game is over, it is nice to talk about ways that helped to find the star. Sometimes body language will come up, but often students will say that they "just knew".

Activities for School Age

Yogi Says

THIS GAME IS A TAKE-OFF ON SIMON SAYS

Pick someone to start the game. The idea is that the leader will say "yogi says....." and add a pose after says.

Everyone will be listening for "yogi says" and the pose, and will then do the pose.

If the leader says the pose without the words "yogi says" everyone should stay in the last pose that was said with "yogi says."

If they did the pose when there was no "yogi says" said, they can stand in the middle for one turn in a chosen pose like "Tree Pose."

Or they can stay in the circle and do a forward fold for one round. (just some suggestions!)

The idea is to have fun even if you make a mistake!

Activities for School Age

Yoga Adventures

Materials: yoga mats, your Imagination

This is a great way for kids to help make the yoga class their own and be involved in what they create. Adventures can be for any theme. You can have an adventure to the beach, a farm, a city like New York, or a country like Australia.

The adventure can also be to a brand new place that kids make up, like fairy castles or Lego land. The sky's the limit with this activity. Because this is a free-form activity, the script can change as quickly as kids come up with ideas.

Be ready to think on your feet. If someone says they see a one-eyed monster, have the kids make up a pose for a one-eyed monster. Be flexible and creative. The real key is to have fun!

Some fun adventures are:
The beach, the forest, the zoo, the farm, Alaska, France, New York City, Fairy Castle, A Magical Island, Lego Land

Activities for School Age

Videos of adventures:

Yoga Adventure to the Plains Indians

https://www.youtube.com/watch?v=7i PpeTQuJ10

Yoga Adventure to the Beach

https://www.youtube.com/watch?v=aupXwJP viAw&t=1s

ACTIVITIES FOR SCHOOL AGES

Nature Mandalas

Materials: pieces of nature, paper bags, an area outside where people walk

Kids love mandalas. Weather coloring sheets, mosaic tiles, or this version, they are all fun and build in the idea of mindful attention.

When we take mandala creation outside, we can also bring in the concept of impermanence -nothing lasts forever and it is okay to enjoy what we have now!

Before you start this activity, giving some background about mandalas is nice.

There are some awesome YouTube videos that show the creation processing Tibet.

Here is one of my favorites:

https://www.youtube.com/watch?v=IYVcjFhpsHc.

If you are lucky enough,

you might also be one of the cities the monks journey to, creating mandalas, sharing their culture, and promoting world peace.

A visit to one of their ceremonies is well worth the time!

Image property of Janice Pratt

Activities for School Age

Directions

Give everyone a paper sack. When you head out for a nature walk, instruct everyone to pick up as many different things as they can find in nature. It can be anything they find on the walk, as there are always some man-made items to find along the way. When everyone has their bags full, head back to the area where you will create the mandala and dump out the things they have found.

As a team, they get to decide how their mandala will look. What goes in the middle? If you have similar objects, how should they be used? What patterns do the objects go in?

When you are finished, you can do a ceremony or a loving kindness meditation. Ask everyone to notice what the mandala looks like the next day. Notice the changes.

Games for School Age

Tall Tree, Small Tree

Materials: space

Tall Tree, Small Tree is a yoga version of Red Light, Green Light.

Directions

Pick one student to start the game. Everyone else goes across the room and stands in a straight line, facing the student who will be "it."

The student that is "it" will turn their back and say in a loud voice "Tall Tree, Small Tree, 1, 2, 3." They can say these words fast or slow.

When they have finished, they turn around quickly.

When the person that is "it" starts saying "Tall Tree, Small Tree, 1, 2, 3," everyone in the line begins to move toward "it."

When she/he turns around, they have to freeze in tree pose. If the person who is "it" sees them move, she/he can send them back to the starting line.

Repeat this process until one student gently taps the person who is "it" on the back before she/he turns around. Then start the game with a new "it."

Games for School Age

Cat, Snake, Dog

This game is a version of rock, paper, scissors.
I learn from "Rainbow Kids" Yoga.

Divide kids into pairs to start. They will hold out one hand flat and make a fist with the other hand. They will lightly pound their hand and say "Cat" or" Snake" or "Dog," then call out one word after 3 pounds. In this game, Dog beats Cat, Cat beats Snake and Snake beats Dog.

The winner of the round does their winning pose (cat, snake, or dog) and then runs off to find a new partner.

The loser goes to one of the open challenge cards and does the challenge. When they are done, they go off to find a new partner. You can put on some fun music as kids play. Play until you feel the game is done!

Images Courtesy of Canva, Public Domain

Games for School Age

Cat, Snake, Dog

CHALLENGE CARD

Do "5" regular or knee push ups

GAMES FOR SCHOOL AGE

Cat, Snake, Dog

CHALLENGE CARDS

DO "10" Jumping Jacks

GAMES FOR SCHOOL AGE

Cat, Snake, Dog

CHALLENGE CARDS

Do "10" Chair Squats

GAMES FOR SCHOOL AGE

CHALLENGE CARDS

Do “5” Dolphins

GAMES FOR SCHOOL AGE

Cat, Snake, Dog

CHALLENGE CARDS

Do "20"

Mountain Climbers

GAMES FOR SCHOOL AGE

Cat, Snake, Dog

CHALLENGE CARDS

Do “10” Lunges (each sides)

Activity for School Age

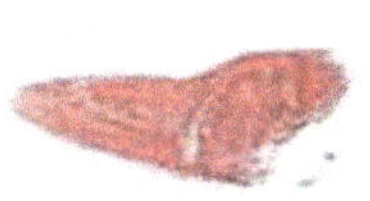

Affirmation

Materials: Index cards or sticky notes

Affirmation Scavenger Hunt

Affirmations are super powerful things we say in the present tense.
Take index cards or big sticky notes and have them
ready in front of you with your favorite crayons or markers.
Think of 3 things you want to tell yourself.
These can be things you want to be true or already know to be true.
Write them on the note-cards
(younger kids can draw and adults can help with writing).
These can be things like:
"I am amazing at playing soccer."
"I am going to do great on my math test"
"I move through life calmly."
After you get these great affirmations together,
tape a small treat* to each note. Now parents,
it is your job to hide the notes around the house.
When the kiddos find the notes, before they can have the treat,
they have to do their favorite yoga pose (make one up if you
don't have a favorite)
and say the affirmation 5 times!

Treats may be edible, but could also be a coupon for an
extra book at bedtime, a trip to the park, etc.

Activity for School Age

Affirmations Continued

There are many powerful affirmations you can use.
Affirmations are a great way to reaffirm how great we are!
Here are a few examples to get you started:
"I am strong and brave."
"I am smart and confident"
"I love who I am."
"I am a kind person."
"I am a great brother/sister."
"I am kind to others.
"I am happy."
"I am good at helping at home."
"I am good at learning new things."
"I am good at cleaning my room.
"I am a team player."
"I help my friends."
"I am a good soccer player."
"I am special."
"I am proud of who I am becoming."
"I am good at my jobs."
"I am beautiful."
"I am good at taking care of my pet."
"I am good at riding my bike."
"I am good at playing games with my family."

Activity for School Age

Body Sock

Materials: Body Sock

Body socks were designed to help children who have sensory issues but are fun for all kids.
They are made of a super stretchy material that fits over the body.
They also come in different sizes, including sizes for adults.

Directions

Have a student put on the body sock.
Other kids can sit in a semi- circle around the student who will wear the body sock.
The student who will wear the body sock can choose to have their head in the sock or outside of the sock.
When they are inside of the sock, they will do a yoga pose.
Have other students try to guess what pose they are doing.

Check out the link to find out the cost of body socks:
https://a.co/d/4eBOPSw

Image Courtesy of Janice Pratt

Activity for School Age

Ball Pass with Feet

Materials: balls of different sizes, mats, a large space

Directions

Start by having students form one long line with their mats.
They will lay on their mats from head to foot Start with a
medium size ball at the foot end of the line.
This person will grab the ball and hold it between his feet
Without using their hands, this student will reach the
ball over their head to his neighbor's feet.

This student will grab the ball with his/her feet (no hands) and continue
to pass the ball down the line.

Variations

At the end of the line, reverse the direction of the ball travel.
Form a circle laying down head to feet, and pass the ball with feet
around the circle. Use different size balls.
Place feet on the wall with hips close to the wall, lying side by side.
Pass the ball down the line of feet
Younger kids, sit in a circle and pass the ball with feet side to side.

Activity for School Age

Chocolate Games

All of these activities can be done with chocolate of non-food items can be substituted.

Option 1 (for older kids)

Give everyone a plastic spoon and a Hershey's Kiss.
Place the kiss on the spoon and then place the handle in your mouth (but too far).
To do some yoga poses without having the kiss fall on the ground.
If it does fall, students just pick the kiss up and place it back on the spoon!
You can also use a pompom on the spoon instead of a kiss.

Image Courtesy Janice Pratt

Option 2 (all ages)

Relay Races

Create two teams and have the kids race against each other:

- crawl with a kiss on their back
- crab walk with the kiss on their belly

Activity for School Age

Rocket Pose or Volcano Pose

WE CAN OFTEN COMBINE POSES TO MAKE FUN WAYS TO PRACTICE YOGA.

Rocket Launch

Start standing in mountain pose.
Slowly come down with knees together and see if you can balance on your toes.
If you can hug your knees with your arms, that can help with the balance.
Pretend that you are launching like a rocket.
Countdown-5, 4, 3, 2, 1.
Launch yourself up to the sky, ending in Mountain Pose!

Volcano Explosion

Start standing in mountain pose.
Slowly, come down with knees together and see if you can balance on your toes.
If you can hug your knees with your arms, that can help with the balance.
Pretend that you are a volcano getting ready to explode.
Feel the lava getting ready to come up to the
surface in one big burst of energy.
When you have all that energy built up, launch all that lava and
steam to the surface as you jump up as high as you can.

kk

Activity for School Age

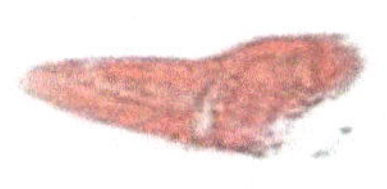

Kindness Hearts

Materials: 4x4 Sticky Notes or construction paper, index cards or other craft paper.

Prep: if working with younger children, you might want to cut out hearts ahead of time or have a template handy.

Decide on how many hearts you would like to start with (5 is a manageable starting place, but you can grow this project as much as you like).

On each heart, think of a compliment or word of encouragement that you can give to someone you care about.
Some ideas might be:
"I love how you shared your snack with me," to a brother or sister.
"You are the best artist I know" to a friend.

Once all the hearts are made (decorating the hearts is an option too), have kids give them out to the people they made them for.
If a hug is appropriate for the person they are giving them to, that is a great mood booster!

(*We know that one hug boosts the feel good hormone "oxytocin" and can make us all just a little bit happier.*)

Discussion: How did it feel to make these for people?
How did it feel to give these to people?

kk

Activity for School Age

Kindness Hearts

Material: none

Name Games are a great way to start new classes.

It helps build community and gets everyone to meet their classmates.

Directions

Have everyone stand in a circle.

Tell everyone that they are going to spell their name using their bodies.

They will have a few minutes to think of a shape for each letter of their name,

and then they will teach their name to the group.

At the end of each person showing their movements that go with their name, have students say:

"Nice to meet you........

"Welcome to yoga......

or

"Shanti,……..

Games for School Age

Bean Bag Games

Material: bean bags

Name Games are a great way to start new classes.
It helps build community and gets everyone to meet their classmates.

Directions

Option 1

Have everyone stand in a circle.
Tell the group you are going to create a pattern by tossing the bean bag across the circle to someone while calling their name.
The goal is for the person to be able to catch the bean bag so you are tossing gently, underhanded.
The person who was called will catch the bean bag, call out a new name, and toss the bean bag to that person.
Each person may have only one turn.
The last person will toss the bean bag back to the first person.
Repeat the pattern throwing it back to the same person.
When everyone has the pattern down smoothly, add in a second, third, or more bean bags.

John

Sally

"Bean Bag Name Game" continued

Option 2

Using the same directions as option 1, have everyone make the circle bigger.

This will require that the throws are more accurate, that people are making eye contact with their partner, and saying their name loudly.

Option 3

When everyone is familiar with Option 1, add a more difficult layer to the game.

First, create the pattern so that everyone knows who they are throwing the bean bag to.

Next, have everyone start walking around the room.

Whoever has the bean bag will call out their person's name, find them in the room, and toss the bean bag.

Add bean bags as the skill level increases.

Teacher's Note:

Teacher's Note:

Yoga Games and Activities for Teens/Tweens

Creating a Show

Materials: a knowledge of yoga

Showing what you know is always fun for teens and tweens.
They are many options for creating a show and these can be recorded or done live for an audience.
It is fun to let the students plan the program.

Option 1

Have students work in pairs to create a series of poses (5-7) that they will do facing each other. They will do their poses at exactly the same time, matching pace and movement.
Each group of 2, will stand in a row, so that it looks like 2 rows.
When the music starts, have the pairs start their poses.
As you look down the line of students, you get a kaleidoscope effect of yoga poses.

Image Courtesy of Janice Pratt

"Creating a Show" Continued

Option 2

Have students plan a class with each student taking a section to teach. Record the class and share with families.

Option 3

Plan a family class where the kids come up with the crafts and games they will do with their parents and siblings. Let each teen choose what they would like to teach.

Games for Teens/Tweens

Design a Pose

Materials: creativity

This game can be done in pairs or individually and just requires some creativity.

Directions

The directions are so simple and kids have so much fun with this activity. It can be done with a variety of age groups, also.

Each team or student's job is to create a brand new pose that has never been done before, give it a name, and then teach it to the group.

If working in teams, everyone in the team must be a part of the pose!

"H" Pose- created by our students, adapted by us!

Balancing Figure 4

Flying Team Pose

Images Courtesy of Janice Pratt

Activity for Teens/Tweens

Eye-Gazing

Looking into someone's eyes at first can be uncomfortable, but it can help build compassion and understanding of others.

Version 1

Face your partner.
Look at each other closely for 15 seconds.
Notice 3 things about that person.
After that time, share what you noticed with the other person while looking into their eyes.

Version 2

Sit facing your partner.
Set a time for speaking - 30 seconds to a minute.
Give out a question.
Have the first person speak about or answer the questions for the allotted time while looking into the eyes of their partner.
After the time, have the listener recount the information they heard.
Now switch.

Version 3

This time have each partner look at each other for a set amount of time, without speaking or moving.
When the time is up, have each partner share how that felt.

Activities for Teens/Tweens

Gratitude Journals

Materials: paper, colored duck tape or other decorations

Gratitude journals are a place to record all the things in your life that you are grateful for.
We know that when we focus on the positive in our lives, our brains become stronger at making positive connections.
There are many ways to make journals from, construction paper covers filled with lined paper to pre-made notebooks that are decorated with a variety of materials.
Teens especially like colored duck tape. Pull out the decorations and be creative.
Having connection with your journal can make it exciting to fill with gratitude.
Gratitude list:

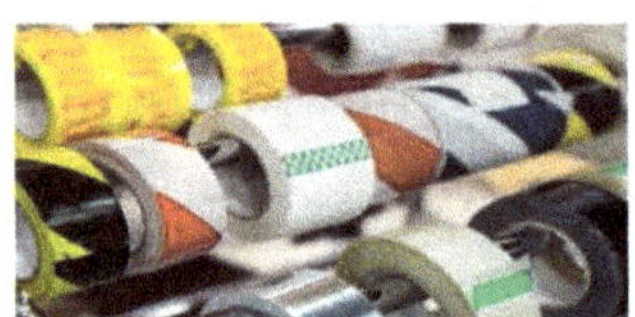

Games for Teens/Tweens

Group Counting

Materials: have students sit in a circle

This game requires patience and impulse control, in addition to observational skills.

Directions

This game can cause quite a bit of frustration, initially. After a bit, however, students can work together to make it really fast and efficient Have students sit in a circle. Count the number of students in the group. Tell students that their goal is to count out loud from 1 - 20 (if this is the number in the group). They can't start with one person and just go in order around the circle. The numbers need to be called out in popcorn fashion. Each person can only say one number. After someone has said a number, they are done until the game starts again. If two people say a number at the same time, the group must start over with "one." When students are just learning this game, the teacher usually starts the game by saying "one:" however, as the students get better, you can make this open to someone in the group.

Activities for Teens/Tweens

Minute to Win It Games

Material: each activity requires a different set of supplies

Minute to Minute Games can be researched on the Internet. There are thousands of different ideas. The games I chose are fun, build community, have challenges, and often require focus and attention.

Activity 1

Hersey Kiss Race

Materials: Hersey Kisses, oven mitts

Divide students into 2 groups and have them form 2 lines. Have the students stand at one end of the space and place a pile of Hersey kisses at the other end of the space.

Give each team a set of oven mitts to put on.

Each student will have one minute to run down and unwrap as many kisses as they can with the oven mitts on.

I let the kids eat the kisses if they get them unwrapped, but of course that is up to you!

I also let everyone have a kiss at the end of the game just for fun.

"Minute to Win it Games" continued

Activity 2

Balloons in the Air

Materials: balloons

This is an individual challenge, so each student needs two balloons. The challenge is to keep the two balloons in the air for one minute without holding either balloon, but by tapping it to keep it in the air.

Activity 3

Thread the Spaghetti

Materials: Box of Spaghetti and a box of Penne, table.

Each student gets one piece of spaghetti.

Spread the penne out so they are on the edge of the table.

The students will put the spaghetti in their mouth and without using their hands, will try to thread the penne onto the spaghetti for one minute.

"Minute to Win It" Games continued

Activity 4
Pencil Bounce

Materials: Pencils with erasers, large plastic cups

In this challenge, students must bounce the pencil (its eraser end) onto the floor and it must land in the cup.

They have one minute to see how many they can get into the cup.

Activity 5
Golf Ball Balance

Materials: two golf balls per student

The goal here is to see if while holding one golf ball in one hand you can get the second golf ball to balance on the first golf ball.

They have one minute to get it balanced.

Activity 6
Ping Pong Bounce

Materials: bucket, ping pong balls

Students will try to bounce the ball on the floor and get it to land in the bucket.

They have one minute to get as many as they can in the bucket.

Make up your own! It is super fun!

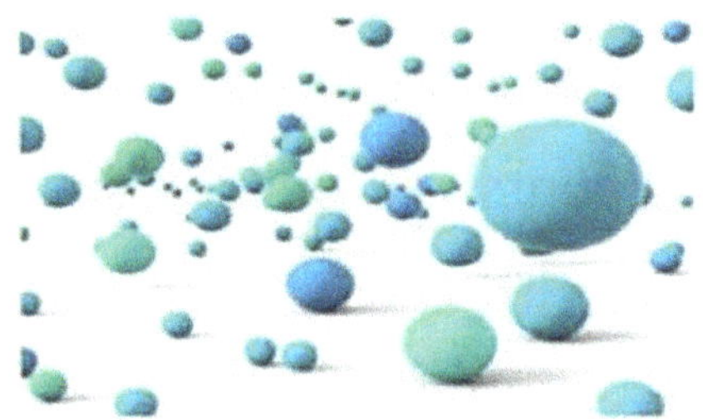

Activity for Teens/Tweens

Peace Flags

Materials: cloth, fabric markers or permanent markers, string

Peace Flags can be created with many different themes. You can have students learn about the Tibetan flags that were hung in the mountain passes to offer safety to those passing through the mountains, or you can have students design their flags around a theme. When they are done it is fun to display them for others to see.

Directions

Cut cloth to measure approximately 5" x 7".

I have gotten sheets from the thrift store and cut those up. Fold the top of the cloth over and sew it to make a flap to run a string through. Give everyone an idea of what you would like them to draw on their flags. Maybe the theme is to draw some place that makes them feel peaceful. Maybe you ask them to draw what they love most. Allow everyone to create and string the flags up for everyone to enjoy.

Image Courtesy Janice Pratt

Activities for Teens/Tweens

Practice Teaching

Materials: a knowledge of yoga

This age group loves to show what they know and to take on leadership roles. Teaching a yoga class is a great way to develop this leadership. This gives you a great way to talk about the flow of a yoga classes, what elements you include and why - breath, movement relaxation, and to talk about themes - gratitude, strength, balance, stress relief. You can have students teach just part of a class to start - the breath or 5 different poses in the movement part of class - and build up to them teaching the whole class. This is a picture of 3 teens who went through a formal yoga teacher training program to become certified yoga teachers.

Games for Teens/Tweens

Rolling Wave Teen/Tween Games

Material: none

This game is fun to video so the kids can see how it looks when they do it as a team. When watched, it looks like the students are creating a spiral with their bodies.

Directions

Have everyone stand in a line facing the same way, shoulder to shoulder. It is not necessary to hold hands but preferred. This helps to keep everyone connected as they begin to move. Starting at one end, the last student will begin to 1-roll'" their body toward their neighbor, pulling the next person along with them. The line will begin to move, forming a rotating circle. When everyone is in the circle formation, 11" or 2'" people will be in the middle with everyone else wrapped around them. Now reverse the process. Watch this video for a better understanding:

Rolling wave.

https://www.youtube.com/watch?v=zJMV5dzGWYO

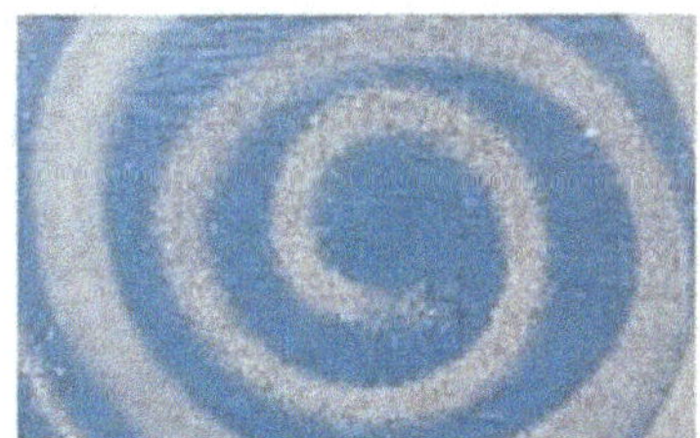

Activities for Teen/Tweens

Service Projects

Materials: a knowledge of places in the community that need support.

This age group can be very creative when given the task of "helping others."
In yoga, selfless service is called "seva."
It is the idea that you do something for others without the expectation that you receive something for your service.

Some great project ideas are:
Collecting blankets for an animal shelter collecting food for a food bank Pennies for schools to help build schools in impoverished areas collecting books to go to a library Christmas toy drive Mitten drive for a shelter Clean up a local park
Start a community garden.

These projects do take time, commitment, and energy to make them successful, but can be so rewarding and a great experience for kids.
Here are some good resources for information:
https://www.goodcharacter.com/service-leaming-web-resources/
https://www.edutopia.org/topic/service-leaming
https://designersforleaming.org/service-learning-resources
https://youth.gov/youth-topics/civic-engagement-and-volunteering/service-learning

Activities for Teens/Tweens

Thorn, Bud, Rose

Materials: have students sit in a circle to share

This is a sharing activity that can be used at the beginning or ending of class. We have adapted it a bit because we like to start and end class on a positive note.

Directions

You are going to go around the circle and have each student share their thorn, their bud, and their rose about a particular situation. It can be about their day in general, or you can get more specific.

Thorn: Share something that is bothering you about your day. Maybe something that didn't go well or like you had planned.

Bud: Share something that you are working on or something that is just starting to make sense to you.

Rose: Share what is the highlight of your day. What went really well?

Activities for Teens/Tweens

Care and Connect

Materials: works best in a circle

Care and Connect is an activity that helps students think about others. You can use this activity with any number of themes. The idea is to just share something in a positive way. This activity is also a great way to allow everyone to have a voice in the group without judgment.

Directions

Have everyone sit in a circle.
Take your left hand and place it on your left knee. Take your right hand and place it on the left hand of your neighbor's hand.
Pick someone to start. In some cases, it might be the teacher of the group. Whoever starts will also pick the theme.
For example:
"Today I would like everyone to share one thing they are grateful for about the class we had today." The first person might say:
"I am grateful for the laughter and fun we had today."
After this person says this, she will take her right hand and pass this thought to her neighbor by moving her right hand over to the left and tapping her neighbor's right hand. Now, it is the next persons turn.
Continue round the circle.

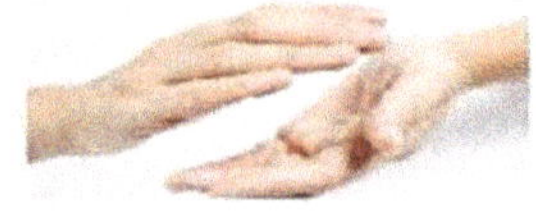

Games for Teens/Tweens

Pass the Hoop

Materials: hula hoop

Pass the Hoop is a game where neighbors have to work together to pass a hula hoop around the circle.

Directions

Form a circle and have everyone join hands. During this game, you are not to let go of hands. The idea is not to break the connection in the circle. Pick a place to start and add in the hula hoop. (Of course, they'll have to unhook hands this one time!) With the hula hoop, they need to pass it around the circle so that it gets back to the place it started. It is up to them to decide how to move the hoop, but in most cases, it works to have students put their heads through the hoop and then step through with their feet

When students get really good at this, you can add in a second hula hoop or a smaller hula hoop!

Images Courtesy of Janice Pratt

Activities for Teens/Tweens

Chanting and Singing

Materials: recorded music, a harmonium, or just your voice

A voice teacher of mine once shared, "When we all sing together, our breath and heart rates sync." Chanting is singing together with the purpose of getting in touch with ourselves and those around us. The ancient mantras that are chanted in sanskrit activate pressure points in the mouth, in addition to stimulating the chakras. There are mantras for just about everything - healing, opening doors, releasing fear. If it is something you are interested in, you might find a local kirtan event and give it a try.

Option 1

Modern Songs

Make a favorite song an opening or closing song for your class. Songs like "Let There be Peace" (https://www.youtube.com/watch?v=bgL1v8FZaNM&t=125s) or "It's a Wonderful World" (https://www.youtube.com/watch?v=rBrd_3VMC3c) are very yogic!

"Singing and Chanting" Continued

Option 2

Learn a Simple Chant

Lokah Samastah Sukhino

Bhavantu

(https://www.youtube.com/watch?v=0CUDrTIXwOA)

May All Beings Everywhere find peace and happiness

and may I be instrumental in making that happen.

Activities for Teens/Tweens

Human Shoot

Materials: a big space

This is a fun activity that requires teamwork and direction following.

Directions

Have all but one person lay down on the floor with head and feet going the same direction. You will lay close together with arms extended overhead but so that arms are touching. You want everyone's head to be at about the same level across the line. The person who is not in line will stand at the front of the group. The goal is to get the standing person all the way to the other end of the line like he/she is on a human conveyor belt.

The start person will get down on her knees and extend her arms. When the teacher says go, she will push forward to come laying on her belly on the people on the floor. At the same time, the people on the floor will start to roll together toward the end of the line. As they roll, the start person will begin to move down the line until she is pushed off the last person.

Key factors: everyone must roll together until the top person is past them. Everyone has to stay close together, arms touching.

The person on top must stay straight

Image Courtesy of Janice Pratt

Activities for Teens/Tweens

Somatic Exercises

Materials: none

Research has shown that the body holds experiences. The holding can feel like tension, stress, or even illness. Somatics is the area of movement study that uses release techniques that target the body and nervous system to restore balance.

Activity 1
Heal Drops

Have students stand up. Start by noticing the feet as they touch the floor. If they are comfortable with the idea, have them remove socks and shoes. Sway side to side and front to back and then find a place where it feels like your feet are balanced with all sides of the feet touching the floor.

Now rise up on the toes, hold for just a breath, and then let the heels fall to the floor. Let this be a release of effort and not a slow lowing. The heels will feel like they are pounding on the floor.

Repeat for a few minutes and then come back to the swaying side to side and front to back.

Find center again.

Notice how you feel.

Activity 2

Arm Swaying

Stand with feet apart, slightly more than hip distance. Start by rotating the body side to side in a twisting motion, allowing the arms to gently slap the body in the front and back of the body. Continue side to side, swaying and tapping the body. You can have students then raise the arms to shoulder height, tapping each shoulder with each rotation.

Images Courtesy of Janice Pratt

Activity 3

Moving Together

Have students stand in a group. One person (maybe the teacher) will start by swinging one arm front to back with the other arm going in the opposite direction. After students see the movement, have everyone else start to swing their arm at their own pace. After a few minutes, tell everyone that you are going to start moving together one person at a time. Moving to your right, the person next to you will make their arms move with yours - right to left and front to back. Then the next person to the right will come into sync. Move around the circle like this until the whole group is moving together. After a few minutes, drop the arms. Close the eyes, and notice any sensations. Discuss how this felt.

Image Courtesy of Janice Pratt

Crafts for Teens/Tweens

Lotus Craft

Materials: lotus pattern, tape, markers

The lotus flower symbolizes how sometimes we struggle through difficult times but can come out with something beautiful from that struggle.

Directions

Using the pattern, cut out 9 petals and one lily pad.

Write a word that describes what you are grateful for, onto each petal (or draw a picture).

Or something that makes you happy when you feel sad.

Or something that makes you feel safe when you are afraid.

You can make the first 4 things you are grateful for in yourself. Maybe you are strong. Or funny. Or kind.

The next 5 can be things outside of yourself that you are grateful for. Maybe your family, friends, teachers, your home, your pet, etc.

"Lotus Craft" Continued'

When the petals are finished, you are ready to put them together. Lay the 4 petals side by side. Lay the other 5 side by side the same way. Connect (glue, tape, or staple) petals at the bottom and form a ring. Repeat with the 5 petals, making a slightly larger ring to place outside the inner ring. Arrange the lotus petals on the lily pad. Keep this at home to remember all that we have to be thankful for.

With small kids (or large classes) you will want to cut out the petals and lily pads before class and hand them out. Older kids can trace and cut their own If you want to make the colors simpler (for less problems in choosing their colors) you can make all the lotus flowers multi-colored (different colors for the petals) or bring all one color of paper for the petals.

Images Courtesy of Janice Pratt

Activities for Teens/Tweens

Check-in Activities

Materials: gather everyone in a circle

Check-ins are a way to find out what is going on with your group. It gives each of the kids a chance to share something about themselves if they want to and helps build connections in the group.

Option 1
What is your Weather?

Sitting in a circle, ask the kids to think of how they are feeling right now and compare that to a type of weather.

If they are sad, they might say they feel like a gray, rainy day.

You can come back to this activity at the end of class to see if anyone's weather has changed.

What Kind of Car Are You Today?

Here we are looking to find out about energy level in the class.

Ask everyone to compare their energy level to a type of car.

For example, if they have a lot of energy they might compare themselves to a Ferrari.

Again, you can come back to this comparison at the end of class to see how energy levels have changed.

"Check-Ins" Continued

Option 3

One Word Check-In

You could have a theme for your class and ask everyone to give one word that goes with the theme. For example: you can ask everyone to say one thing they are grateful for if the theme is gratitude.

Option 4

Introduce a Topic

Have students give a short response to a questions you propose. For example: "Do you feel that you should always tell the truth?"

Option 5

Open Ended

Ask students to say something that went well that day or week or something that went wrong. These can become themes for class or ways for students to clear the space before class begins.

Teacher's Note

Teacher's Note

Find your SUPERPOWER!

Image Courtesy of Janice Pratt

About the Author

Jan Pratt has been a "yogi in training" for the past 25 years. She found that yoga was a great complement to gymnastics, dance, and hiking, and that a yoga mat could travel anywhere!
She has been fortunate enough to train at yoga ashrams in both Austria and Germany. She is 200 RYA trained, trained in Accessible Yoga and Karma Kids yoga.

Jan has also been passionate about children for most of her life. While raising children of her own, she has also owned a preschool, been a children's librarian, and worked in public schools.

Jan is currently busy writing a series of books designed to empower children to pursue their dreams.

For more information on her books, visit: www.janpratt.com
"Children are natural yogis-ready to explore their world with their mind, body, and spirit. Join us and play!"

www.omtastic-yoga.com

www.ingramcontent.com/pod-product-compliance
Lightning Source LLC
LaVergne TN
LVHW081421110826
845149LV00010B/1829

9798988793625